COLLECT]

Crombie

TO DO WITH R.C.S.

In a thrum of
the breathings and percussions
of music, and surrounded
by fish and
ideas – the one
as slippery to grasp
as the other – he plunges carefully
into people. When he comes out,
they're softened, he's toughened.

How many hands must a man have
to hold all he wants to hold
without juggling?

Norman MacCaig

COLLECTED POEMS

Crombie Saunders

with a preface by Donald G Saunders
and an introduction by Ian Spring

Published 2022
by Rymour Books
45 Needless Road
PERTH
PH2 0LE

https://www.rymour.co.uk

ISBN 978-1-7398466-6-4

Cover design by Ian Spring
Typeset in Bembo
Printed and bound by
Imprint Digital
Seychelles Farm
Upton Pyne
Exeter

A CIP catalogue record for this book
is available from the British Library

The paper used in this book is approved
by the Forest Stewardship Council

CONTENTS

From *XXI Poems*

From *This One Tree*

PREFACE

In so far as Robert Crombie Saunders is known these days, it is as someone who was part of the so-called Scottish literary renaissance of the twentieth century, a phenomenon whose significance is still a matter of debate, but which without any doubt saw fine and important work produced. As a journalist and editor, most notably of *Scottish Art and Letters* and the *Selected Poems of Hugh MacDiarmid,* Saunders had a role in the wider renaissance, but first and foremost he was a poet.

Compared with most of his contemporaries, Saunders's poetic output is small. The three volumes he produced in his lifetime are long out of print, and apart from the occasional specimen in Scottish verse anthologies (though not the latest ones), his work is largely forgotten. This collection sets out to remedy that. Of course, neglect is no signifier of merit, often the opposite. However, I strongly believe these poems deserve to be better known, or at the very least available — and not only to scholars of the period but to anyone who enjoys poetry. In the end, as always, it is the reader who will judge.

My father was born in Glasgow in 1914 to a family inordinately blessed with schoolteachers (father, grandfather, uncles), something which may have influenced his later career choices. His ancestral roots were Dumfriesshire, Fife and Aberdeen. He attended Glasgow High and Hillhead and studied English at Glasgow University, graduating MA in 1937. From 1938–39 he was an assistant editor with the publishers, Blackie & Son. Ruled medically unfit for military service, he was employed during the war as private secretary to David Archer, publisher, and as an employment officer in the Ministry of Labour and National Service.

In 1944 he edited the *Selected Poems of Hugh MacDiarmid,* arguably the first critical collection of the great poet's work and one which was credited with reviving and sustaining MacDiarmid's reputation during the war years.

Between 1944 and 1948 he was editor of the annual *Scottish Art and Letters*, along with J D Fergusson as Art Editor.

Saunders's first poetry collection was *The Year's Green Edge* in 1955, followed soon after by *XXI Poems*, which contained most of his poems in Scots. From then on, his work would appear only in anthologies and poetry magazines until 1986, when he brought out *This One Tree*. Privately published and circulated among friends, this comprised most of the poetry since the fifties as well as earlier uncollected pieces.

Politically, Saunders aligned with the left and with Scottish independence. This is clearly reflected in his journalism. From 1947–59 he was associate and literary editor of the left-wing newspaper *Forward,* pursuing a Scottish Nationalist line for the Scottish edition somewhat at odds with that of the editor, George Thompson. (Their friendship survived this, if not the latter's ennoblement). In 1953, shortly after the death of Stalin, Saunders was part of a cultural delegation to the Soviet Union. He was, briefly, editor of the *Scots Independent* (1953–54), but left after quarrelling with the then SNP Chairman Dr Robert MacIntyre over the matter of editorial independence.

Other than literature, Saunders's main interests were music, particularly jazz (he played a righteous blues piano) and fishing. In fact, he became something of a professional angler. He edited *The Scottish Angler* (1948–53), the only journal of its kind at the time, compiled *A Guide to the Fishing Inns of Scotland* (1951), and was Angling Correspondent for the *Daily Herald* from 1954–57. In 1958 he became a short story assessor and children's books reviewer for the BBC.

From 1952, Saunders was working out of Tomnavoil, Balquhidder, a tiny cottage in the Perthshire Highlands he had moved to from Glasgow. With a growing family to support, he took the decision to retrain as a schoolteacher. He taught first at Balquhidder Primary, then Killin Junior Secondary, then McLaren High, Callander, where he was part of the English department until his retirement. His last years were spent in Killin, Perthshire.

Crombie Saunders was a friend and supporter of many of the major players in the Scottish Renaissance, including Sydney Goodsir Smith, Sorley McLean, Douglas Young, Alexander Scott, C M Grieve (Hugh MacDiarmid) and, in particular, Norman McCaig, who he introduced to Christopher Grieve. However, chronic ill health and geographical isolation meant that Saunders was never a regular with the Rose Street crowd. His friendships were conducted through correspondence and visits rather than propping up the bar in the Abbotsford or Milnes. Also, they included others not of that circle, such as J F Hendry and Moray McLaren. Ian Hamilton Finlay was another close friend. Towards the end of his life, he renewed his acquaintance with the poet W S Graham, and they exchanged regular letters and audiotapes of their work.

The poems are in the order in which they appear in the three publications. In the case of *This One Tree*, this is far from chronological. Later 'free verse' poems rub shoulders with earlier formal ones. Having been unable to date many of the poems here with any certainty, I have taken the option of repeating the original arrangement.

Regarding the poems in Scots—or Lallans, as he aligned with the movement of that name—Saunders by and large followed the guidelines of the Scots Style Sheet produced by the Makar's Club in 1947, and which he was himself involved in. They were published in 1955 without a glossary but included here is a brief one containing some of the less well-known (and sometimes idiosyncratic) Scots words.

Finally, this is the 'Collected Poems', not the Complete Poems. There are other pieces,* some juvenilia, some incomplete, some in draft form only. But I am as confident as I can be that all the poems Saunders wished to be known by are here.

* In his younger days he wrote dozens of comic verses and parodies. Many of these appeared (under a plethora of pseudonyms) in *Glasgow University Magazine,* which he edited, between 1933 and 1937. While these show a whole different side to his talent they are, along with his journalism and prose, outwith the scope of this book.

Donald G Saunders, Gartmore, 2022

NOTE: The cover painting of Crombie Saunders, by the Scottish artist William Crosbie, is reproduced here with the kind permission of Paolo Rossi.

INTRODUCTION

The poems in this collection are of such quality that it is surprising they have been out of print for so long—especially considering that the work of Crombie Saunders (correspondence shows that he seldom employed his first name, Robert) was admired by so many of his contemporaries. In fact, no higher an authority than Hugh MacDiarmid writes to him on 31st of March 1944: 'I have read your own collection with great interest and much pleasure, and will look forward to its publication. You handle the Scots very effectively and most of the verses have wit, pith, and grace of expression.'[1]

It is unclear which poems exactly are referred too, (although they would probably be Saunders's Scots poems which largely appeared in the collection *XXI*). However, it was to be a decade before his first published collection of poems appeared. In the interim he was busy, on top of his employment as a journalist and an editor, and a schoolteacher from 1952, with a variety of literary endeavours (despite ill health which dogged him, notably the effects of a perforated duodenal ulcer and burns suffered in a house fire). His friend Norman MacCaig emphasises his versatility in his poem 'To Do With R C S':

...How many hands must a man have
to hold all he wants to hold
without juggling?[2]

The most significant efforts of his early literary career were to be associated with the enterprising Glasgow publisher William (Bill) MacLellan, who published a variety of important books on Scottish literature between 1941 and 1969. In 1944, Saunders edited *The Selected Poems of Hugh MacDiarmid*, published by MacLellan.[3] This is the first substantive collected edition of the poetry of MacDiarmid containing a selection of verse from *Sangschaw* (1925) through to *The Islands of Scotland* (1939).[4] It, along with the American anthology *Speaking for Scotland*, undoubtedly led to the cementing of MacDiarmid's reputation through the war years.

That Saunders was anything but a passive editor is demonstrated by the fact that the normally self-reliant MacDiarmid wrote to thank Saunders for advice on his use of Scots.[5] Saunders notes in his introduction to *Selected Poems*: 'Readers familiar with the earlier texts of the poems in Scots will notice that certain orthographical changes have been made in the present edition. These alterations have been made by me with the approval of the poet.' In fact, Saunders, MacDiarmid and others were contributors to the debate regarding 'plastic Scots' that took place in the letters columns of *The Scotsman* during 1946.

Saunders's selection of MacDiarmid's poems is, as he stresses, a personal one. But there is little doubt it is the shorter poems in Scots that he favours:' ...Scots lyrics where MacDiarmid's power is at its purest and most intense. These short poems from 'Sangschaw' and 'Penny Wheep' have greatness in small measures which is rare in degree and quite unique in kind. In them the freshness of MacDiarmid's use of the Scots conveys his peculiarly immediate vision with startling clarity, and poems like 'The Man in the Moon' and 'Empty Vessel' have a universal quality that makes them become, inevitably, an important part of the reader's experience. The proof the contemporary lure of Scots as a literary language may safely rest on these lyrics: no language in which such poetry can still be written can be ignored.'

In the same year as this publication, MacLellan launched a new periodical, *Scottish Art and Letters*,[6] with Saunders as the main editor (J D Fergusson was the art editor and MacDiarmid is credited with editing one edition).

Scottish Art and Letters ran until 1950 and its philosophy is exemplified in Saunders's introduction to the first edition in which he clearly sets his stall:

> Too often the Scottish artist has succumbed quite unconsciously to the idea that all critical standards have their locale in London and must necessarily continue to do so; consequently, lacking the support of others who differ from the English tradition similarly to himself, he inclines to arrive cap in hand at the back door of the English capital and, however he may rationalise his acts, accommodate himself to its requirements. The result is too often a drastic limitation of his range…
>
> The fact that individual artists occasionally arise who do not allow themselves to be diverted by conditions and criteria antipathetic to their particular statements is rather more than is deserved by a country which rewards their integrity by complete indifference. It is true that little opportunity exists for their work to obtain a hearing, but when the work is there and its importance evident it seems to be paradoxical that the people of this and other countries should be unable to enjoy it merely because it does not conform to the dictates of some other culture. It is hoped that 'Scottish Art and Letters' will, by collating different aspects of contemporary work, cancel this deficiency to some extent.
>
> The revival in the artistic life of Scotland is of course most developed in literature where in addition to writers of such generally recognised achievement as Edwin Muir, Hugh MacDiarmid, etc, we find distinctive work being done both in the short story and in poetry; of the younger writers in these genres in English a very large proportion are Scottish, not only in birth but quite markedly in the orientation of their work.
>
> In addition to the poets of such groups as the 'New Apocalypse', seventy per cent of whom are Scots, there

are numerous other Scottish poets of considerable worth writing in Scots, Gaelic and English who are not associated with any group or movement. While poets confining themselves to work in English have several reputable magazines in which they may and do appear with some regularity, poets writing in the Lallan or in the Gaelic are in the unfortunate position of having little chance of appearing in a review published outside of Scotland and therefore at the present time little chance of appearing in a review of any standing whatever.[7]

His nationalism and passionate defence of Scots as a medium for expression is emphasised in a later editorial in which he berates an 'English reviewer' who 'recently described Mr MacDiarmid's extraordinary achievement [of the] birth of a new literary Scots as a squandering of his powers on the childishness of attempting to resurrect the language of Dunbar... ' He continues:

As already stated, many of the younger Scottish poets are at present writing mainly or exclusively in Scots, and this is an enterprise which 'Scottish Art and Letters' will be glad to encourage. Whether English is not even for the English in a state of exhaustion is a question which must be considered in the light of the many rather desperate forms of experimentalism which much of the most important contemporary work in it has taken; certainly for the Scottish writer it is not, and never has been, a medium in which he could draw upon the vast reserve of national experience. which would inform a really adequate literature.[8]

The scope of the contributions to *Scottish Art and Letters* cannot be overstated. Contributors include the writers Hugh MacDiarmid, Eric Linklater, Sydney Goodsir Smith, Douglas

Young, Sorley MacLean (referred to by the Gaelic version of his name, Somhairle MacGhilleathain), Robert MacLellan, Maurice Lindsay, Ewan MacColl, William Montgomerie, George Campbell Hay and Fred Urquhart.

The world of art as represented in the journal included prose and visual contributions from, among others, the artists J D Fergusson, William MacTaggart, F J Peploe, E A Hornel, Donald Bain and William Crosbie (who painted the portrait of Saunders that is featured on the cover of this book). All in all, the journal featured nearly all the prominent protagonists in the world of Scottish art and literature at the time.

Saunders himself contributed comparatively few poems to *Scottish Art and Letters*. However, apart from the editorial input, he contributed reviews that demonstrate the range of his reading. His own criticism is wide-ranging and could be most witty and acerbic. He writes of Auden, 'It is Auden's awareness of man's isolation that has always given his poetry its power. The lack of development of his poetry, as of the poetry of Eliot, is one syptom of the spiritual chaos resultant on that isolation'. And here is a review of *The Cosmological Eye* by Henry Miller: 'Henry Miller, I am afraid, has a callow mind. It is his implied ambition to have no mind at all… but inexorably, reality caught up with him.'[9] His reviews also demonstrate an acquaintance with Joyce and Proust and contemporary art.

Two things are clear. Firstly, that Saunders had been writing poems himself throughout the period of his involvement with Scottish literature from at least 1944 onwards. Secondly, that during that period he had been extensively involved with contemporary Scottish literature and had a wide appreciation of literature on an international stage. Both influenced his poetic output.

Before examining the texts of the poems themselves, however, I want to mention two aspects of Saunders's writing practice that are evident, if not from his early work, at least from his later work.

Firstly, he was constantly working on the structure of his verse. He discusses a poem, 'Hostess', in a letter of 1st of October 1969 to an unknown recipient:

> I enclose for your interest, and I hope, enjoyment, a copy of a poem I have just completed. As you will see, the first line of each stanza is an iambic pentamenter (with a whatever-is-the-opposite-of-catalectic one in stanza three) and the next and the next two short lines are also ten syllables but in syllabic style. It seems to me an interesting pattern, and I hope it works. Stanza four bothers me: lines two and three are metrical. In the strict pattern they shouldn't be: but I like the movement and am unwilling to force them into the free verse form.[10]

The poem, benefitting from his considered alterations, is contained within this volume.

Secondly, it is clear that he worked tirelessly on the editing of his work. One example, pictured here contains his amendments to 'Thinking of Hugh MacDiarmid'.

Also, he would work on the titles of the poems. The poem that gives the title to the collection *The Year's Green Edge*, published here as 'An Elegy for the Glory and the Dream' was published in the collection as 'The Year's Green Edge'[11] but was originally published in *Scottish Art and Letters* as 'The Second Holiday'.

I will now look at some of the poems by Saunders in English.

'Above the Formidable Tomb' is ostensibly a poem about the crucifixion of Christ, but many of the more general themes that can be found in Saunders's work can be found here: love, death, nature and the changing of the seasons. It also illustrates Saunders's concern with form. In essence, the structure is vertically based on the contrast between the lines '*Above* the *formidable* tomb' and '*Below* the *lamentable*

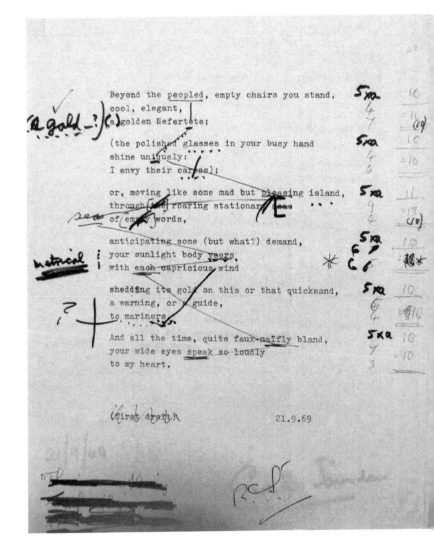

Beyond the peopled, empty chairs you stand,
cool, elegant,
(a) golden Nefertéte;

(the polished glasses in your busy hand
shine uniquely:
I envy their caress);

or, moving like some mad but pleasing island,
through the roaring stationary seas
of empty words,

anticipating some (but what?) demand,
your sunlight body veers,
with each capricious wind

shedding its gold on this or that quicksand,
a warning, or a guide,
to mariners.

And all the time, quite faux-naïfly bland,
your wide eyes speak so loudly
to my heart.

(first draft)   21.9.69

This manuscript page features the poem 'Hostess', a work that seemed to exercise Saunders for some time due to uncertainty about its structure. The notations include counting of syllables in each line.

THINKING OF HUGH MacDIARMID

Cocooned in cloth, with leather
Slapping the stone paving,
~~You mover your tremulous~~ column — *his ~~soft foot~~ man-high*
Of soft flesh, jigsaw bones,
Skilfully packaged guts and
Pounding blood, imprpbably
Vertical, through acres
Of unimportant landscape.

What makes a man'an instrument?
That people meet him, ~~and~~ protest:
"He wasn't God: he blew his nose!
Tripped on the step. Di̇ he write those?"
- "It's an achievement of the ~~trrrrx~~ mind;
Inspired? An idiotic word!" -
While, Chris, your nonsense I respect,
I never doubt your intellect,
But - ~~honestly, how was it~~ intellect
~~That~~ laid a girl's hand on the crucifers?
Or saw in the dark sacrifice of roots
The necessary price of beauty? Bards
Are judged by what they do, not what they are,
And you, being a materialist, would approve.
~~But~~ what you are, we love, in what you've done,
~~A~~ greatness even greater than your own.

        o   o   o

"In my nature," said Christopher Smart,
"I quested for beauty,
"But God hath sent me to the sea for pearls."
You've dug since, MacDiarmid,
In many black, wet tunnels,
In ~~the~~ sweaty detritus of a brutal toil,
Hiding your bright body
In a decent Sunday black;
Or, edgy in the sun,
Have scratched and chipped at harsh stone,
Clinging to belief in case the quarry
Should ~~become~~ only a place and not a thing.
I respect but do not pity your condition,
Your mind inflamed with metaphor, your lungs
Choking with phlegm of parables and syntax.
What's garnered is sufficient, and the peril
Ephemeral at the end; a noble end,
To suffer and die among
Elusive minerals.
Thinking of Hugh MacDiarmid,
I think of any miner and his shovel.

This manuscript page features the poem 'Thinking of Hugh MacDiarmid', one of Saunders's best works. The various annotations demonstrate his meticulous attention to editing and improving his work.

cross' (my italics). Here is the poem in full:

Above the formidable tomb
No angel will be known;
And where Earth's child is buried, there
The void protects its own.

Spring had a smile of hyacinths
In the morning of the year,
Whose transitory innocence
Knows no revival here.

Her innocence could not foresee
That sullen death would give
To an ecstatic enemy
His own prerogative.

Below the lamentable cross
The weeping mother stands;
And love, for which her child had died,
Lies useless in her hands.

Love and nature are two predominant themes in, at least, his earlier poems. 'The Aberdeen of Desire' seems to be a poem about a love affair. The first verse employs an oxymoron comparing the grey granite of the city with the heat of passion:

In the provincial cold
Of a north-east drifter station
I am suddenly appalled
At the bitter blast of passion,
Here where sombre granite holds
The sun's ecstatic grin.

And the last verse nails the contrast cleverly:

> And now my frolicsome fettle
> Is broken by the glamour
> Of your little face, like a petal
> Plucked in this north sea summer,
> Into the final and fatal
> Aberdeen of my desire.

Poems often feature little epiphanies or fatal moments, as in 'Tomorrow the Station':

> The question falters
> Gravely on this moment,
> Whether your troubled love
> Will find in crisis courage;
> Or whether indecision
> Will conquer, and my journey
> Leave no excuse for caring
> And more than fields between us.

The protagonists in some of these poems often seem helpless in the unfolding of their own fate and Saunders, who often evokes the natural world, stresses this in his poem 'The Mole', in which the creature, innocently, remains unaware of impending death:

> Under the frozen leaves the small beast turns
> And strains at a task it does not comprehend,
> Its muscles taut with destiny, and joy
> In its sightless eyes. But O, the time is short
> Already the raven lifts a tattered wing
> And flies to meet its shadow on the crag.

The natural world is also evoked in 'The Derkened Universe', a poem stylistically reminiscent of MacDiarmid's early lyrics that Saunders so admired:

> The eident licht endlang the simmer yird
> Liggs sairly on a hert that canna see
> Beyont the shaddaw in the valley's breist
> Whaur daith has twin'd your luveliness frae me.
>
> The laverock wi sunsheen in its tongue
> Sings vainly for a hert that canna hear
> Abune the sough o branches in the wuid
> A music that wad tell me you were near.

However, the personal also develops into the more general as in 'You Spoke of Seasons':

> We lay down on the grass
> And loved because we must,
>   And the ironic trees
>   Regarded with unease
> Your sweet and innocent lust.
>
> But time's barbaric lust
> Has laid the mountain low
>   And emptied of its flowers
>   The valley that was ours
> Two hundred worlds ago.

Developing the contrast of youth and age bracketed by nature and time fully, 'An Elegy for the Glory and the Dream' displays a controlled lyricism that is perhaps most reminiscent of the work of Dylan Thomas:

Here is the hill that in the summer solstice
Knew my delight, where on a windless day
I still would hear a planetary music
That sounded through the organ of its pines,
Till suddenly I climbed out of the trees
On to a summit bare beneath the clouds,
And watched the river winding far below
And felt the young earth turning in the sky.

But what in the mountains are my dreams today,
In this precipitous land, this place of ravens,
Where sheep indifferently crop away
The eyes and lips of the world's childhood face?

Fully developed, Saunders's evocation of land and time becomes a commentary on Scottish history as in the poem that is most often referred to as his best, 'The Empty Glen':

The hamlets failed, the young men sought the towns,
Bewildered age looked from the cottage door
Upon the wreck of all they'd laboured for,
The rotting gate, the bracken on the downs;

And wondered if the future was so black
The children would have stayed but did not dare,
Who might, they hoped, be happy where they are.
And wondered. Are they ever coming back?

In *The Mainstream Companion to Scottish Literature*, Trevor Royle notes:' ...his poem about the effects of the Clearances, is a reminder of the care and attention devoted to language and metre by this poet, who published all too little... '[12] The Clearances seem to have been a particular interest of Saunders, as in *Scottish Art and Letters* he enthusiastically reviews Fionn MacColla's *And the Cock Crew.*

Saunders's influences are various and his poems take different forms. An interesting piece is 'Connacher's Lament for Deirdre' based on the Irish legend that is best known perhaps as 'Deirdre of the Sorrows'. And the poem can be seen as influenced by William Butler Yeats.

Saunders's poems in English as discussed have great merit but he was equally skilled in writing in Scots, or Lallans, as he expressed it. His poems in Scots were largely published in the collection *XXI* in 1955.[13] His knowledge of Scots is clearly extensive and there are verses herein in different forms: Middle Scots and Standard Habbie, a form favoured by Burns.

If the influences on his poetry in English were, perhaps, MacDiarmid, but most likely other Scottish poets such as Edwin Muir and Norman McCaig—a particular friend—the influences on his Scots poems is various. He was resident in Perthshire at the same time as William Soutar who, bedridden from an early age, was also not directly part of the Edinburgh Rose Street set. It seems that Saunders never visited Soutar at his house in Wilson Street, Perth (although he was familiar with his work and his son recalls him reciting Soutar's bairn sangs) but it is obvious that there is common ground in their work and Joy Hendry notes the influence of Soutar on Saunders's poems in English. However, it seems to me that is more similarity between the Scots poems of Saunders and Soutar. Here is 'Had I Twa Herts' by Saunders:

Had I twa herts and you bot ane
Whan we were twin'd, still for your sake
That I micht luve yet be alane
Ae hert wad thrive, the ither break.

Had I twa tongues to speak o thee
I cuidna let a morrow come
An hearna o your cheritie

From ane—the ither wad be dumb.

Compare it to these lines from Soutar's 'Gin Ye Had Come Last Nicht':

Gin ye had come last nicht
Wi' the thochts o' ye that cam,
Ye wudna no be what ye are
Nor I be what I am

Gin ye had come last nicht
Whan my thocht was but ae thocht,
It wud hae been anither sang
That you an' I had wrocht.[14]

Saunders, it seems, continued working on new poems, but there is a hiatus in publication after 1955. In 1969 he is submitting poems to Robert Nye at the *Scotman*, but without success. However, there was to be one final publication, *This One Tree*,[15] privately printed in 1986. The dedication is 'to the Memory of W S Graham, a fine poet and a dear friend.'[16] Saunders corresponded with Graham and they also exchanged audio tapes of readings.

One poem in this collection had previously been published in 1967, in a collection of poems for Hugh MacDiarmid on the occasion of his 75th birthday edited by Duncan Glen, the editor of *Akros*. This is 'Thinking About MacDiarmid', in which he returns to old ground:

What makes a man an instrument?
That people, meeting him, protest
'He wasn't God: he blew his nose!
Tripped on the step! Did he write those?'
—'It's an achievement of the mind;

inspired? An idiotic word!'—
While, Chris, your nonsense I respect,
I never doubt your intellect,
but was it only with your intellect
you laid a girl's hand on the crucifers?
or saw in the dark sacrifice of roots
the necessary price of beauty?

Earlier, he had written, in a review of MacDiarmid's *Lucky Poet*:

It is difficult to read widely in MacDiarmid's very varied writings without realising that the fundamental impetus in his work derives from an emotionalism to which his ratiocination is subsequent and subject. One feels that if the trend of the argument were to lead too clearly to an unbelieved conclusion the whole argument would quickly be, brought to heel and, if it were not amenable to discipline, rejected as unstable in its premises. This is another way of saying that MacDiarmid is a poet... explaining by logic an experience which is itself the proof of its own validity, no doubt to placate a certain suspicions racial streak of Lowland down-to-earthness. Because there is clearly evident in MacDiarmid's own make-up something of the antisyzygy which engrosses him in the national scene.

In the final verse, the antisyzygy is expressed in the contrast between his personal friend Christopher Grieve and the 'grand old man of letters', Hugh MacDiarmid:

I think of Christopher Grieve;
with reverence, astonishment,
exasperation, pride, some disapproval,
timidity, delight, a disbelief,

amusement (pardon!), maximum respect,
regrets, gratitude, homage and love.
Thinking of Hugh MacDiarmid,
I think of Christopher Grieve.

Perhaps MacDiarmid's complex character and the variety
of his work perhaps provided opportune subject matter for
other poets but this particular poem bears an interesting
comparison with Hamish Henderson's 'On Reading Lucky
Poet':

You tilt against 'Englishism': the words sleek and slick,
The smoothing fingers that add trick to trick;
The admirable refusal to be moved unduly
By the screaming pipe. The desire to speak truly
With a middle voice; the acceptance of protection;
The scorn for enthusiasm, that crude infection...
That's all very well.
But what about 'Scotchiness',
This awful dingy bleary blotchiness?
You list 'Anglophobia' as your recreation,
But it's Scotland that's driven you to ruination![17]

It is clear that Saunders and Henderson both had interesting
and complex relationships with MacDiarmid. They also
had in common an interest in European poetry and both
translated from Heine and Hölderlin,[18]

Crombie Saunders, despite his health problems, had
a variety of interests including music[19] and angling[20]
on which he also wrote over a period of time. In fact,
his fishing adventures were not unconnected to his
poetic endeavours and his frequent companion was
Norman McCaig and another great friend, the artist and
writer Ian Hamilton Finlay, contributed short prose pieces
to a journal he edited, *The Scottish Angler.* Despite these

other endeavours, however, Crombie Saunders did produce a substantial body of work that is a significant contribution to Scottish literature that can be partly measured by this new collection.

The quality and variety of the poems in this collection are both striking and Donald G Saunders, the son of Crombie Saunders and a poet in his own right, should be congratulated for presenting them to us. However, he stresses that they are not the *complete* poems of Crombie Saunders (although he notes '...I am as confident as I can be that all the poems Saunders wished to be known by are here.') For example, 'The Exile' is a poem in the form of a sonnet published in the first edition of *Scottish Art and Letters*. However it is one of two titled 'Two Sonnets' and the former of the two contained therein, unlike the latter, was apparently not chosen by Saunders for his published collection *This One Tree*, published forty-two years after the original publication in *Scottish Art and Letters*. The same edition of *Scottish Art and Letters* also contains a short poem in Scots, 'Pricksang', which is also not contained herein.

Therefore, there is more scope for research into the work of Crombie Saunders and this brief introduction may inspire further scholarship.

NOTES

1. National Library of Scotland MS. 26799.
2. This poem is from a private letter to Crombie Saunders and is not included in Norman MacCaig, *Collected Poems* (London: Chatto & Windus, 1988).
3. Hugh MacDiarmid, *Selected Poems* (Glasgow: William MacLellan, 1944).
4. See Alan Bold, *MacDiarmid* (London: Paladin, 1990), p. 446.
5. National Library of Scotland MS. 26799.
6. *Scottish Art and Letters* ran between 1944 and 1950. Not to

be confused with another journal of the same name published between 1901 and 1902.

7. The 'New Apocalypse' was a name given to given to a group of poets who first appeared in an anthology of the same name edited by the Scottish poet J F Hendry.

8. In a later edition of *Scottish Art and Letters*, Saunders writes: 'The poet, the novelist, and the dramatist are as essential to a full and healthy life as the sailor, the engineer, and the farmer; for a country is poor indeed that does not cultivate the arts as warmly as its commerce and its soil. We are therefore confident that we are acting not only in the interests of Scotland, but with the sympathy of all who understand the proper needs and aspirations of humanity and a living nation... One of Scotland's leading writers (R L Stevenson) and one of the greatest writers of partly Scottish blood (Hermann Melville) both put on record strong expressions of protest at the way in which the structure of life in the Western 'civilised' countries in which they lived, cribbed, cabined, and confined their creative powers.'

9. Interestingly, as he was developing as a poet, Saunders sent work to both Eliot and Auden and received them back with annotations.

10. In the same year he writes to another correspondent: ' ... here are some recent poems. The latest is 'Hostess', a play with iambic pentamenters followed by two lines of syllabic verse, also ten syllables. In the middle, when I describe the damn woman's body moving around the room (I wish they wouldn't: it begins to bother me), I switch to metrics and replace the two syllabics with iambic pentameters. Then back to the former pattern. I think it works'. National Library of Scotland MS. 26799. Clearly he had decided that it worked as evidenced by the poem in this collection.

11. Robert Crombie Saunders, *The Year's Green Edge* (Baltimore: Contemporary Poetry, 1955). Published under the auspices of the journal *Contemporary Poetry* to whcih he had contributed a poem, 'In the Loneliness of a Classic Dispensation', in 1944 (although that poem was not added to the collection.

12. Trevor Royle, *The Mainstream Companion to Scottish Literature* ((Edinburgh: Mainstream, 1993), p. 266.

13. R Crombie Saunders, *XXI* (Edinburgh: M Macdonald, 1955)

14. W R Aitken (ed.) *Poems of William Soutar: a new selection* (Scottish Academic Press: Edinburgh, 1988), p. 217.

15. The title of *This One Tree* is ostensibly taken from the poem 'The Encounter'. However, Donald G Saunders believes the title to be another reference to Wordworth's 'Ode': ' …But there's a tree, of many one,/ A single field which I have looked upon,/ Both of them speak of something that is gone. Typescripts of 13 of the poems from *This One Tree* can be found in the National Library of Scotland National Library of Scotland MS. 26799.

16. Saunders was a frequent correspondent to a variety of writers in Scotland and further afield. For example, they included A S Neill of Summerhill school.

17. Three of his translations appear in Tom Hubbard (ed.) *The New Makars : the Mercat anthology of contemporary poetry in Scots* (Edinburgh: Mercat Press, 1991). All of them plus new 'translations' by his son, Donald G Saunders, were published in Robert Crombie Saunders & Donald G Saunders, *Twal poems duin ower intil Scots frae the German o Heinrich Heine* (Gartmore: Tomnavoil Press, 2019). Donald Saunders makes clear in his introduction that he regards these as adaptations rather than translations: 'These are not translations. Translation (*übersetzung, owersettin*) demands a depth of knowledge of language and context that neither I nor my late father could claim.'

18. See Hamish Henderson, *Collected Poems,* edited by Corey Gibson (Edinburgh: Polygon, 2019). For an longer analysis of this poem, see Ian Spring, *Hamish Henderson: a critical appreciation* (Perth: Rymour, 2020).

19. Saunders's interest seems to have been mostly in jazz, but one incident relates to Scottish traditional song. In the 1950s Sydney Goodsir Smith wrote to him: Regarding the Ball of Kirriemuir… Recently I have a letter from an evidently mad but amiable Americans in Paris called (oddly enough) Legman. Gershon Legman was a noted folklorist who worked with

Hamish Henderson and others. He writes copiously about the song in a later work without referring to any contemporary Scottish sources. See Gershon Legman, *The Horn Book* (London: Jonathan Cape, 1970) pp 157-424 passim.

20. He wrote *A Guide to the Fishing Inns of Scotland* (London: Nicholas Kaye, 1951). A revised and expanded edition was published in 1977.

21. Outwith the scope of this collection are the short stories written by Crombie Saunders. Several, written from the 1930s onwards, are preserved in the Mitchell Library, Glasgow (ref: J000160921): An ordinary man, Spiders in the Morning, Man of Letters, Return to the River, A Nice Change, The Sisters, Thirty Pieces of Silver, A Pound of Ling, Nellie is my Darling, Deirdre, Willie, There's a Towel in my Coat, Duet, Dennis Nicol, who always did what he was told. Saunders had been a short story assessor for BBC Scotland and, along with another query, (about the writer J Fullerton Miller), he sent these stories to Hamish Whyte in 1985. They were too late for Whyte's edited anthology, *Streets of Stone*, but Whyte, a librarian, asked they they be preserved in the library. His other literary endeavours include the editing of a humorous magazine containing short prose pieces aand cartoons entitled *Ploy*. It seems that two issues of this were printed by William MacLellan, one immediately before and one immediately after Worl War Two. However, only the latter seems to now exist. Also, perhaps surprisingly, from 1945 to 1948, whilst he was editing *Scottish Art and Letters*, he was also the editor of a glossy fan magazine, *Film Feature*.

from

THE YEAR'S GREEN EDGE (1955)

WHO WALKS WITH PLOVER

Who walks with plover
On pedantic moorland,
Sure and aware
Where curlews carve the ordinary sky:
This valley is his personal affair.

Who flies with chat
At sundown, like a lost
Ghost but again
Training desire, a gun, on to the moon:
Morning will find him still an alien.

Who tends his plot,
Weeds beauty like a garden,
Guardian of his trees,
Sees death behind the swallow like a friend;
Knows his loved enemy. Neither of these.

THE SELF-LOVED

You talk with crowds and walk in crowded rooms
And act as though your death were any man's,
Knowing it never was so near a hand
And that the wound was never quite the same.

And still within your brain the hammers fall
Upon the minutes of a private time;
And voices cannot penetrate your smile,
And emptiness grows round you like a shell.

ABOVE THE FORMIDABLE TOMB

Above the formidable tomb
No angel will be known;
And where Earth's child is buried, there
The void protects its own.

Spring had a smile of hyacinths
In the morning of the year,
Whose transitory innocence
Knows no revival here.

Her innocence could not foresee
That sullen death would give
To an ecstatic enemy
His own prerogative.

Below the lamentable cross
The weeping mother stands;
And love, for which her child had died,
Lies useless in her hands.

THE BOTTOMLESS GULF

Walking along a lane
The wheels of a cart had rutted
I compared the certainty of my step
On the edge of a three-inch canyon
To the terror and constant danger
I would know if instead of three inches
The drop were a thousand, although
The physical risk were no greater.

So you who walk on the brink
Of a life beyond all conception
Are secure, seeing no drop
Or at most a slight declension.
But look down and observe
The bottomless gulf beside you
And then, if you still are able,
Walk on the lip with assurance.

THE ABERDEEN OF DESIRE

In the provincial cold
Of a north-east drifter station
I am suddenly appalled
At the bitter blast of passion,
Here where sombre granite holds
The sun's ecstatic grin.

I had hoped it might expire
Travelling in Holland,
Fishing the shores of an empire,
—Or at least if I got on some island.
But no, it followed me everywhere
With the blare of a brass band.

It began to appear like a friend,
Or a most unwelcome companion,
This perpetual fragment of sand
In my subtle and delicate engine.
The visitor came unexpectedly and
Made menacing each dawn.

And now my frolicsome fettle
Is broken by the glamour
Of your little face, like a petal
Plucked in this north sea summer,
Into the final and fatal
Aberdeen of my desire.

MISUNDERSTANDING

The casual cow in the circumstantial landscape
Is for the moment my reality,
Through the window of the frightened present
Time is a number of snapshots without any sequence.
Travel my habit, my only virtue patience,
I have mislaid my ticket and no longer believe in stations

But you, my darling, the sun behind your shoulder;
Lost in a sort of grateful loneliness,
Sit with your back to the future
And watch the well-behaved past receding like fields;
Terrified by (and hoping the friendly porter will
  guard you)
The great anonymous valley racing toward you.

And so we share unwilling and troubled silence;
Refusing the past, the word you await would
  betray me
And shatter your poise like a sudden crash into buffers
At the end of a siding.
                    Therefore, on guard,
I offer you now, like the tickets they'll soon be demanding
And for ever my caring and careful misunderstanding.

TOMORROW THE STATION

Tomorrow the station
And the separate friendly people,
Crowding the doors and exits
With their visions and needs and baggage;
And for me the slow breath of doubt
And hunger for conviction,
The rails to horizons leading
Or ominous, pointing to panic.

The question falters
Gravely on this moment,
Whether your troubled love
Will find in crisis courage;
Or whether indecision
Will conquer, and my journey
Leave no excuse for caring
And more than fields between us.

TO A DON

Part of your heart was Saturday to me.
The dialectic lecturer in Greek
Stuck on your tongue to watch the flowers speak,
Unfriendly. But your sad eye couldn't see
Jeevy and Dinny bending on the shore
To watch an old man dressed up as a crab;
Your party-line perception, shouting 'Scab!'
Had mined that province for a different ore.

No, what you wanted was a big mistake
To settle like a pigeon on your wrist;
Your dogmas thundered frequently, but missed.
So now your moon is dark, your sorrows take
Leave of their sense to give the lucky school
Part of your heart that's Saturday to rule.

THE EMPTY GLEN

Time ticks away the centre of my pride
Emptying its glen of cattle, crops and song,
Till the deserted headlands are alone
Familiar with the green uncaring tide.

What gave this land to gradual decay?
The rocky field where plovers make their nest
Now undisturbed had once the soil to raise
A happy people, but from day to day

The hamlets failed, the young men sought the towns,
Bewildered age looked from the cottage door
Upon the wreck of all they'd laboured for,
The rotting gate, the bracken on the downs;

And wondered if the future was so black
The children would have stayed but did not dare,
Who might, they hoped, be happy where they are.
And wondered. Are they ever coming back?

YOU SPOKE OF SEASONS

You spoke of seasons when ambition sped
Over the youthful ocean with delight
Your hopes into the land I tenanted,
And when it found no anchorage in sight
Endured the weary platitude of days
Till love at last sailed slowly homeward bearing
Unwilling dreams like wide-eyed emigrés
That found no harbour in their sad sea-faring.

But also learn how, haunted by their sighs,
My heart became a ship; its singing deck
Swung through the stars into a new sunrise
In glad pursuit.
                              And found your love a wreck
With crippled sails, upon the ocean tossed,
Its precious cargo in the deep sea lost.

INNOCENCE

How quiet my love lies, hidden in the weed
Where waters eddy round her murdered heart;
Pity with all its power cannot part
This poor Ophelia from her lonely deed.

So gently cruel death becomes the light,
So innocently plunders innocence;
The voice, bewildered, stumbles into sense
Its magic echoes buried in the night.

The doom is dark for one whose raucous day
Shouts folly on his dearest discontent;
And still two voices speak, that represent
Reason and intuition; and they say

'O unloved bird, O shattered wingless dead,
The world's despair is you uncomforted.'

THE MOLE

The withered days blow from the shaken branch
And drop on cold earth where the worms feed
On dead memories. Frost silvers decay,
And through the soil of time in a blind hope
Love tunnels with small powerful hands,
The last ally in the time of our defeat.

In every heart the desperate headlamps race
Down the black roads of distrust and fear,
Each bend revealing futures we do not want
And each road ending at a past we dread.
So midnight wheels its cargo through the sky
And not a voice is heard to cry Repent.

Under the frozen leaves the small beast turns
And strains at a task it does not comprehend,
Its muscles taut with destiny, and joy
In its sightless eyes. But O, the time is short
Already the raven lifts a tattered wing
And flies to meet its shadow on the crag.

THE PANTHERS

Within the confines of this room
My thoughts like hunting panthers roam,
In fields outside grey figures sow
Their furrows while the gulls pursue.

Their clamour on the mountain slope
Threatens the immemorial sleep
That guards this valley, as the sheer
Rock-cliffs of an island shore

Guard the small fields. But time will get
Its own revenge. The rotting gate
Swings in the wind, and the disdained
Slow waves will be victors in the end.

And where a mountain stood will rise
The white gulls in their old carouse
— And in my room the panthers drowse
Till on each claw the red blood dries.

A DEATH IN THE HOUSE

One room was filled with silence; there the past
Finally said goodbye, gentle and grave,
Tolerant of the loud defensive words
That in that troubled moment seemed to have
More than the heart to say
Moving through empty rooms that wept with love

To where the body of my father lay
Remote in its own world of space and time.
And in his house I lingered, loth to go
Back to a life that from his lost life came.
Outside the social night
Unlit and hostile lay the long years home.

TWO LANDSCAPES

Their summits hidden in a sky of snow
My thoughts like mountains mourn the summer past,
Caught in the iron mirror of the lake
Their patient ghosts lie undisturbed below;
And patience disciplines my heart
Holding these worlds of ice and snow apart.

The broom now gold against the granite bright
Burns the reflecting river, and the sky
Full of warm summer curves around the earth
And holds the golden flame till, with its light,
My eyes become another sun
Making these worlds of stone and water one.

SONG

Two hundred worlds ago
A field became your eyes;
    Time waited for the kill
    And, up above, a hill
Leaned over in surprise.

The present was our prize
That would not ever pass,
    Your hand with seasons filled
    And generously spilled
Tomorrows on the grass.

We lay down on the grass
And loved because we must,
    And the ironic trees
    Regarded with unease
Your sweet and innocent lust.

But time's barbaric lust
Has laid the mountain low
    And emptied of its flowers
    The valley that was ours
Two hundred worlds ago.

THE CURTAIN

Between my mind and the light
A curtain of black hangs,
It is too far or too late
Although the dark image longs

For one word or one sound
To express the thought 'I am here';
Desire waves a featureless hand
In the unworded air.

What happens outside the ring
Inside becomes a guess;
It may be right or wrong,
In any case

Unknown. And love can shout
At the top of its voice, for where
In this silence is one who ought
To hear or, hearing, care?

WHY SHOULD YOU LISTEN?

The dove with a white heart is alone in your illusion
And Jupiter makes circles round your hand.
You love the mountain, but you have not noticed
The hungry ocean and the drifting sand.

So with this thought into your world of bright
  enchantment
On a day of howling autumn my phrases come,
Shouldering secrets through the gusty midnight,
Muttering love while you sit quiet at home

And wonder when the stars will bring a different
story
Why should you listen? Nothing I can tell
Will matter while tomorrow is your ally,
Or make the ailing dream you wish for well.

FOLLY

I grew my heart into a season's folly,
Ribboned my hair, combed skylarks from the clouds;
My midyear madness made the summer holy
Surrounding your grey-eyed youth with shouting birds.
And I was of your joy the shadow solely,
Priapus' pantaloon, buffoon of crowds.

Autumn surprised with unfamiliar fears.
Walking my past into the earth, your laughter
Shook the bare branches. What is this ghost that stares
Out of the dark wood where the night birds gather?
You cannot see it, for the bright young years
Have dazzled your eyes with a folly even dafter.

SECRETS

A door opens, a door closes;
And nothing passes through except a sigh,
A solitude of centuries that mutters
Meaningless words that don't know how to cry.

Faces with inarticulate eyes
Encounter sadly, know they have not begun
To learn the alphabet. The man is a stranger
To his lover, even the mother to her son.

The desperate power of the poet,
Callously loving, battles with the bruised heart,
And shouts: 'I am listening; why don't you answer?'
And suddenly, it may be, sees with a start

The madman fondling his own psychosis.
A door opens, a door closes.

AN ELEGY FOR THE GLORY AND THE DREAM

I

Listen, one swallow at the year's green edge
Whistles a welcome on a farm in Crathes;
The pines fold back a corner of the world
Revealing my grandmother, surrounded by roses
  and raspberries.

My heart unhardened now, what parody
Of Spring awaits me at a Deeside station?
Once upon a time there was a mountain …
(O deceiving days, deserve to be remembered!)

Caged parrots in the cool rooms of the house,
Tea in the sunny garden, flowered with light;
I watched the clouds, contented to await
Inevitably beauty in the bee-tormented noon;

My young faith unequipped to understand
The certain gain may be impossible,
And the lonely walks in the wood behind the station
The magic prelude to a club-room joke.

Back in the morgue of childhood I respect
The sun's prosaic duty, I approve
The wave of the hill, the river's conversation;
My childhood, dead, presents its simple beauty,

But where is the hope that breathed into its hours,
And drove its veins of summer on to death?

II

Here is the hill that in the summer solstice
Knew my delight, where on a windless day
I still would hear a planetary music
That sounded through the organ of its pines,

Till suddenly I climbed out of the trees
On to a summit bare beneath the clouds,
And watched the river winding far below
And felt the young earth turning in the sky.

But what in the mountains are my dreams today,
In this precipitous land, this place of ravens,
Where sheep indifferently crop away
The eyes and lips of the world's childhood face?

These rocks are wounds, these suppurating crags
Malignant with memory; the fevered clouds
Lament their dead; along the black loch's edge
A curlew tells its hermit elegy.

III

One night when the loneliness of my desire
Beat on the shaken window like a gale,
The heavy evening sky twitching with bats
And all the fragrant shadows wet with owls,

My soul poured forth the army of its love
Out through the open window to the road,

And over doubt like mountains, cliffs of hate,
And all the world around me and between,

Far and too high for any company
Save the soul's longing; and I stayed below
Awaiting unhappily its secretive return.
Thus when the feet of giants trooped in whispers

Into my hungry room they brought no grail
For suffering, no unction for defeat;
Walking around my fear with face averted,
Looking away in silence when I turned.

IV

Excessive joy my heart intemperate
Lavished on lane and cottage, as the seed
Sown confidently in the favoured field,
Has given a barren harvest in the end.

And yet the light of night defined by day
Is now more real because it never shone,
Because this recollected heaven was only
Born in the moment of its final loss.

Look how the child stood staring through the years
Towards a wonder that today he mourns,
That from the future moved into the past
And yet left all his presents unfulfilled,

That, once anticipated, cannot be
Hoped for again, though felt through each long hour:

The world for which love proved inadequate,
The dead heart ever locked against his own.

from

XXI POEMS (1955)

HAD I TWA HERTS

Had I twa herts and you bot ane
    Whan we were twin'd, still for your sake
That I micht luve yet be alane
    Ae hert wad thrive, the ither break.

Had I twa tongues to speak o thee
    I cuidna let a morrow come
An hearna o your cheritie
    From ane—the ither wad be dumb.

Had I fower een an twa to close
    Wi greetin o a hert forlorn,
The ither twa wad see a rose
    Ahint the gairden o your scorn.

Bot I am ane an sae maun find
    An answer til the mysterie:
Dee an forget, or livan mind
    Aa times my troublit historie.

SONNET

Dear nou, gin sic response were aa I kent
As micht intern my life in povertie,
Lackan bot luve, I wad be weel content;
I hadna then this sair perplexitie.
An tho fordelyd langin rocht my hert
Wi thinkin o that ither happy day,
I hadna fund in treason sae apert
Ane servitour wha staw my traist away.

Or gin mysel an luve had ches to flee
Out o thy hert thegither, I wad dree
Mair lichtlie tho my gledness suld be skaith.

Bot och, the ghaist that glowrs in our bed
Is o a bairn wha lang embraced us baith
An nou is rengan in his faither's stead.

THE DERKENED UNIVERSE

The eident licht endlang the simmer yird
Liggs sairly on a hert that canna see
Beyont the shaddaw in the valley's breist
Whaur daith has twin'd your luveliness frae me.

The laverock wi sunsheen in its tongue
Sings vainly for a hert that canna hear
Abune the sough o branches in the wuid
A music that wad tell me you were near.

Warlds frae the lyft hae fled, an sterns gane black
Sen yesternicht, bot anely God can read
In the derkened universe o my tuim hert
What galaxies He ended whan you deed.

THE ERD IN PUIRTITH

Nou the erd crines in puirtith cauld
An burns greet doun ilk snawy scree;
Puir kimmer, bot hir beautie auld
Taks nae account o povertie.

Aa owre the lyft hir sternies grue
An the ferlie mune is cauld as daith,
Bot simmer an the bien nicht nou
Ligg saftly in the warld's skaith

Till winter slake out frae the wuid.
An sae our countrie, auld an dear,
Maun bide the puirtith till her bluid
Sall walken an the saul steir.

THE STEEKIT DOOR

Day eftir day, ilk year wi'out relief
I ken a fecht that is an's na my ain,
Bot shaws in smaa account the strangest grief
That thro man's warld an speerit aye hes gane:
A door frae whilk I maun avert my een
Kennan it aince was barred an maun be sae,
That gin it suld be glanced at wad be seen
Unsteekit nou.
                There is nae ither way
To tak the road we fear micht hae an end
Reachan a goal we darna comprehend.

RESSAIF MY SAUL

A Poem in Middle Scots

My dolour is ane cup
　　Held to my lippis up;
So, Lord, I pray fra out that wae
　　Thy mercie I may sup.
And so fra wantonness contrair
Into thy bountitude preclair
Ressaif my saul, that it gang fre
Fra seiknes and infirmitie.

Alluterlie my neid
　　Me to defend fra deid
Is of Thy luve, and so abuve
　　Is succour and remeid;
Quhy then so brukil and affrayit
Suld I gang in the warldis gait?
Ressaif my saul, that it may dree
No langer sic perplexitie.

My hert and mind tak cure
　　To be Thy servitour,
Nor for my sin can hope to win
　　Thy luve be adventur.
So fra this warldis wayis to gain
The favour of my Soveraine,
Ressaif my saul, and lat it be
At ane with Thy felicitie.

THE SHILPIT MUNE OF AUTUMN

The shilpit mune of autumn
Keeks wanly thro the mirk,
The manse stauns bien an doucelik
In the yaird ablow the kirk.

The mither reads in her Bible,
The lad at the lamplicht stares;
The alder dochter's dwynit,
The yinger lass declares:

'Och, God, sae dowf an langsum
The days gang by for me!
It's ainly at a yirdin
Hae we onything to see.'

The mither looks frae her buik then:
'Nae lass, bot fower hae deed
Sen your faither they hae yirdit
Doun at the graifan-stede.'

Then gantit the alder dochter:
'I'll no be stairvit here;
The morn the laird'll hae me,
He speird an has muckle gear.'

The son brak out in lauchter:
'There's a twa-three chiel at the inn
Can mak a hantle o siller
An'll show me hou it's duin!'

The mither lat flee her Bible
Straucht at his narra face:
'An wad ye be a riever
And bring us this damned disgrace?'

They hear a tap on the winnock,
They see a beckonan wraith:
Outbye stauns their deid faither,
Hapt in his black priest-claith.

(frae Heine)

I DINNA HAUD WI HEEVIN

I dinna haud wi heevin
By meenisters weel kent,
Your een are aa the heevin
That maks my firmament.

The God the parsons prate o —
I ken he is a lee;
Your hert I haud my faith in
An nae ither god can see.

I canna credit Satan
Nor Hell wi aa its smert:
Anely your bricht een glentan
And your cauld black bitch's hert.

(frae Heine)

AN AULD SANG'S IN MY THOCHT

An auld sang's in my thocht
That tells o dule an skaith:
A thane wi luve's distraucht,
Bot luve's forouten faith.

As trowless he maun lichtlie
The dear luve o his hert,
As shamefou he maun richtlie
Regard his ain luve-smert.

He fain wad front the field
An caa them til the stour:
'Let him assay the shield
Wad haud my luve a hure!'

Then brak the mensefou silence
Ainly his ain despair,
Then was his sword's keen violence
His ain hert's adversare.

(frae Heine)

THE HAMECOMIN

Glaidly the boatman sails intil lown wattirs,
Faran frae faurben isles wi guidly hairst;
Forbye mysel wad mak the journey hame,
Bot whatna hairst hae I sauf dule an grame?

O bienlik kyles that langsyne faither't me,
Wad ye redact the torment o my luve?
An wuids o bairnheid, wad ye bring me there
Gin I suld come forpleynit, peace aince mair?

(frae Hölderlin)

BETRAY YOUR FRIENS

Betray your friens, leit lichtlie o the airts,
Hummle the Great Saul til your ain smaa pairts:
God will forgie't. Bot let nae man be
Intrudant on a saikless lemanrie!

(frae Hölderlin)

NOU, KARL MARX

Nou, Karl Marx, ye've had yir turn,
The new synthesis dinna spurn,
Ye ken yir theorists wad churn
    Butter frae spuds,
Whase dialectic heids are purran
    Up i the cluds.

Ye were a wysslik kind o mannie,
Ay takan aathing affa canny,
Yir hous had muckle ruims whaur anny
    Carlin culd bide,
Bot nou ilk biggs his ain wee crannie
    In whilk to hide.

I'm thinkan, man, ye wad be sweirt
To welcome aa the dour an feart
Wha rin, whan their opeenion's speirt,
    Under yir banner
An, gin they see a hurdle, clear't
    In sic a manner.

It's no sae easy to admit
Hou circumscribed's the brawest wit
An hou the last equation's writ
    Gey faur abune us,
Bot jowk the theorem and it
    'll likely stoun us.

I ken yir doctrine's kernel is:
Ilk thesis and antithesis
Resolved, a new equation is

Ripe fir solution,
Nae theoretic synthesis
    Beean a conclusion.

Sae ye'd expect intelligence
To be a jump aheid o sense
An measure up the nearest fence
    To that we're lowpan;
Aften it anely kens that whence
    Our cuddy's cowpan.

Ye'll mind the chiel wha tummled out
A twal-floor windae (an, nae dout,
Wad no be welcome at the fuit,
    Eftir his *faux-pas*)
Bot haulf-way doun was chirpan out
    'I'm all right so far.'

DOUN THE WATTIR WI THE LAVE

Gangan ane simmer day my lane
    Doun by the Broomielaw,
I thocht the sunlicht wad hae taen
    A maist obnoxious gaw
At sic a sicht it limnit plain
    O' barges, tugs and aa,
An trippers by the thousan gaen,
    Paw, bairns, an maw
            (An the wee dug),
Doun the wattir wi the lave that day.

Mindit to leave the ugsome scene
    An tak a tramcaur hame,
Sudden a boatie caught my een
    That had a weel-faurd name:
Endlang the prow was bauldly dicht
    The *Lallans Belle*, her wame
Was packit fou o mony a wicht
    O' guid and orra fame
          To gang
Doun the wattir wi the lave that day.

No injin drave this bonnie boat
    Bot ilk man had an oar,
An Wow! Ye suld hae seen it float
    A hantle frae the shore,
Wi creakan beams an many a dunt
    Ahintward and afore,
An some o'ts mariners gied a grunt
    And ithers gied a roar,

Sae loud,
Doun the wattir wi the lave that day.

Benmaist the prow a laddie stude
    (Maist like a figure-heid)
Aa beard an specs an langtitude,
    Bot Fegs! there was nae need
For sic a roar he thunnert out
    As for our sins he gied
The *Skye Boat Sang* an *Tammy Troot*
    Translatit at high speed
            Intil Ibwo,
Doun the wattir wi the lave that day.

At stroke (he kent weel hou to swat
    Bot sairly hou to feather)
The halo-heidit Maister sat
    An creeticised the weather;
An whiles he gied a muckle splash
    Pit aathing in a dither,
Syne swung his oar up wi a crash
    Micht brak it aathegither
            Intil firewuid,
Doun the wattir wi the lave that day.

A wysslike carle had a trace
    Wi many muckle huiks,
Baited wi ane- an twa-act plays
    Some screivit in ballant-buiks;
He heist aboard aa doun the route
    Braw fush o different sizes,
His neebors were sair pitten out

To see the glitteran prizes
                    Accrued til him,
Doun the wattir wi the lave that day.

Anither luikit at a gless
      Wi drouth an nae affection,
Sen it was tuim; but nanetheless
      He rowed wi circumspection;
Alang the bank a poetess
      Frae Lunnon mad guid speed
To hurl tributes and a mess
      O' laurel at his heid
                    (A D. Litt. tae!)
Doun the wattir wi the lave that day.

An neist a wee renaissance chiel
      Kept up a steady chatter,
Maist o himsel, bot aa his spiel
      Was smothered by the clatter;
An though his oar (some twa fit lang)
      Culd no get near the wattir,
In aa th'abstraklous *sturm und drang*
      It didnae really matter
                    Ane wey or the t'ither,
Doun the wattir wi the lave that day.

Some ither carles were rowan strang
      Bot sat the wrang wey roun,
Some, haund in pouch, aye tell't the thrang
      That they'd start rowan sune.
Forbye my hert was licht to see
      Sae weel an puirly sairt,

The *Lallans Belle* gang warilie
   Intil its proper airt
               (Parnassus, mebbe)
Doun the wattir wil the lave that day.

THE ALBATROSS

Where tides and trade winds cross
Flew Love the albatross,
Till at the mast-head one
Huge pinion framed the sun.

Loosed then my hand the dart
That pierced that noble heart,
The plectrum of white wings
Plucked at the rigging's strings

And shattered on the deck.
They hung it round my neck;
Asked: 'Why did you destroy
What gave you so much joy?'

And O, did guilt conspire
With murderous desire,
That now I turn my eye
Upon an empty sky?

For always night and day
In carrion decay
I carry on my breast
The infinitely blessed.

THE SEPARATING YEARS

The separating years walk round the table
Blind to your eye. My unconcerning talk,
Tuned in to yesterday, ignores the quick
White teeth of weasels biting winter's apple.

Outside the soiled day gutters to its grave,
But mornings are many and the short run kind,
The little deaths unnoticed; on the other hand
This sudden flash-back mutilates my brave

White introspection, and its bleeding limbs
Tell the defeat of love, show triumph time's.

FESTIVAL OF LIGHTS

The chanting figures carry little lights
Towards their God, moving with awkward grace;
A woman places crimson lotus flowers
In supplication on the river-face.

Authoritative drums reiterate
Their anthem to the serpent and the dove:
What word will scatter glow-worms through this night
And set my crimson years afloat on your love?

ONE MORNING

One morning dawn will show you
Approaching on the horizon
Love with a load of laughter,
And sorrow, the sun arising

Will lead you to that breathless
Wilderness of bluebells,
Where time is not the teacher
And hearts are willing pupils

To learn the gay deceptive
Sarabande the wild pulse leaps to;
May my words then be protecting
And my prayers keep you.

THE ISLAND

Lovely in sunlight with the seaweed shingle
Slipping under the retreating water;
Too few the people and the island dying,
Soon the last boat for son and daughter.

The valley veiled in smoke-grey shadow,
Mild is the mist when the smirr approaches;
Unroofed walls can give no shelter,
Bracken on the croft encroaches.

Gates sag and the grey dykes crumble,
Rain on the hearth, the worm in the rafter;
Rabbits live till the night of murder
On fields that remember the children's laughter.

APRIL

A pebbled river brightly falling,
Sea trout in the gravel glide;
I cast my flies, a troubled peewit calling
Above the April field where tractors ride

Down the brown soil. The noonday hums
In the hedges on a tiny wing.
And memory is a jovial clown that comes
Laughing at losses in the green-drunk spring.

ECHOES

Nothing of this is new. The stubborn past
Stands in the wings to take his curtain call
At each half-hearted triumph; on the last
Calamity his elegiacs fall.

I am the man tomorrow always knew,
The road turns back and tells me where to go.
My destination seeks me. What I do
Was done for me a thousand years ago.

Alas, that every jealous moment could
Reveal the boy I was, and show that he's
Still walking in the disenchanted wood
Where echoes whisper through the separate trees.

CONNACHER'S LAMENT FOR DEIRDRE

I.

Throw earth upon the body of my dream
There where it lies oblivious of the day,
In milling soil where worms will eat
The white bones into flutes. How to redeem
The act one did not will? Or to defend
A love that with possessing was possessed?

So many years my thoughts have constantly
Turned to the north, and daggers in my tongue
Self-wounding iterated 'She is young,'
That now tell sadly, unbelievingly,
How at the last her loveliness at rest
With death brings persecution to an end.

My heart rebuked the squandered unearned joy
That shouted triumph in those dangerous glens,
And fanned my hatred with the lies of sense:
'Your winters creak and Naosi is a boy!'
How long I loved with folly for a friend,
Only despair my folly's interest.

II.

Old thoughts are troubled and uncertain. Age
Brings doubt, and I see dimly through my life.
Even the pain has lost its crying rage:
Defeat was the origin and end of strife.

Who will recall an old man, though a king,
Whom envious affection made destroy
The beauty that he loved, without loathing?
Or will not mourn the luckless girl and boy?

But now, life thinning in the blood, I fear
An accusation from a higher throne:
'You held the image, not the actual, dear;
Hating the best. Why not leave well alone?'

I cannot cry: 'Dignity was at stake!
I grew the flower my old hands could not pluck!'
— My honour lies with Naosi in his grave
And Deirdre, dead, shuns my perpetual love.

from

THIS ONE TREE (1986)

THE ENCOUNTER

After waiting so long
Why should this summer be different?
What can this one tree tell me
That a thousand have not said?
    But walking back from the sea
    Past the dunes, at midnight,
    I met again the tall girl
    With dark eyes of revenge.
    And the black moon dipped,
    The tide choked in the skerries,
    She leaned outward from me
    And her breath was louder than the waves.
For a moment the Earth spoke to me,
And I felt once again
The song on my tongue, of rich and golden bells
Crowding the night, a mad and dancing mirth.

REFLECTIONS ON A POOL

In the black peat-hag a pool of clear water
Mirrors infinities of cloud and sky;
The racing Spring, patterned with light and shadow,
Moves over its small screen, so that I lie

Staring as through a lens at immensity
Oddly minute, where almost I discern
Aldebaran and Rigel shining there
And remote galaxies in the fringing fern.

I am a man, a twig upon this mountain,
My life a pool of time which may, I hope,
At least reflect what it cannot encompass:
Become, in fact, an efficient macroscope.

WALKING ALONE IN THE DREAM-LONGED CITY

Walking alone in the dream-longed city
with laughter sounding down the terraces
of bright bazaars that sell the moon for sixpence,
down empty avenues where every step
leads to adventure— suddenly a change:
Bright, clamouring bells that dried the tongue
  with panic.
The night collapsed, the ruined tenements
were lost in a smoking dust. And there I found
the broken doll that was not to be discarded,
the toy drum filled with soldiers, the ghost in the
  wardrobe,
sea-war and shipwreck on the garage steps.
Can it be living in a dying world
is better than dying to create one?
Is better than dying in a living world
with an unobserved apology for intrusion?
Love
bends like a reed in the flood of envy and hate
that leans its waters on this delicate stem.
There is no longer any answer
to the involuntary prayers of the time-tormented,
the mother who hears the front door close on an
  eldest son,
the girl who looks in the mirror with sombre stare,
all those who dread a sudden step in the street, a tap
  on the pane,
the lonely man who sees his hands and cries.
These are my wife, the brother that I love,
my dearest niece, the children of my house.

Because of them, nothing I ever do
will be quite right, I'll laugh with their twisted
  mouths,
my heart grown grey with their corrupted dreams.
There's no escape. We share a common guilt,
a mutual cowardice. Sins unforgiven
(there's no forgiveness now) tie me to them.

Night falls from my hidden city. Light
cuts in a wounding dawn. Our stubborn hands
pick through the rubble, keeping the decent bricks
to build another tenement or school.

REVENGE

'And, if thou wilt, remember';
    And if you won't, my pet,
I've managed to arrange things
    To make sure you don't forget.

You said you'd always love me,
    And really meant it too;
I never promised anything
    I found I couldn't do.

The wind could break the branches
    But never shook the tree;
Your eyes invited glances,
    But no one looked at me.

Your feet were made to fidget
    As men are made to roam;
If I was sad I hid it
    And stayed, my love, at home.

Your heart was like a river,
    A cloud, the drifting sand;
But mine was yours forever,
    A quiet, unchanging land.

So every road you wander
    My constancy will prove,
And every field be bordered
    By the grey stones of my love.

A GUN IS SOMETHING

A gun is something
I've always wanted. Because
I love people.

I know the enemy; he has
a hard square face. Birds
fall silent when he passes;
trees wilt;
the eyes of children
lose their innocence.

Why should I forgive this man?
Just because he's me?

JANET AT THE SEASIDE

Breakers, and grey gulls
Across the crying land;
Blue in the distance, hills;
And, underfoot, white sand.

Gay in summer dress
Sedately Janet walks,
Over the sandy grass,
On to the sandy rocks.

Her pail is filled with seaweed
To hold the various creatures
She intends to study, indeed
One of the attractive features

Of the seaside, she maintains,
Is the way you can correlate
So many specimens
Of marine invertebrate.

Her older brothers paddle
About the silver shallow,
She doesn't care to meddle
With merriment so callow.

Determined Janet goes,
Gay in self-reliance;
I watch, and blink my eyes
Which are blinded by her science.

ONE WAR OR ANOTHER

Vietnam, Korea. Look back
on ordinary people who,
running from bombs
spilled for their salvation, have gathered
out of the wreckage two plates,
a battered table and one cousin by marriage.

I saw this woman, a sort of peasant.
Her cow was dead, a valuable one. So
was her two-year old child. It was the last
of the herd. She might have got
a good price for it. And what can a poor woman do
without a cow?

DON'T TOUCH THIS

Don't touch this

because it's
not to be touched

I know your face and voice
I've trembled at them both, but
no longer

don't touch this

a time comes when even I
can say: that's enough

don't touch this

gardens splutter, young geese
honk through the midnight air
and the owl
croons lugubriously

these are my friends
not you

don't touch this

once there was a chance, you
weren't there, so I could make you
whatever I wished you to be

something went wrong
I hate you

don't touch this

THE MEETING

One day, perhaps, I'll walk along a street,
hiding my face from faces that I meet,
looking in shops when one I know comes by.
Not easy: I'll be careful not to try
being earnest, purposeful, even aware;
and, almost dreaming, recognise the stair.
I'll climb and enter a familiar door
(though one I'll know I've never seen before);
I'll say: 'You finally decided?' And,
rising from my chair, hold out my hand.

AN INTRANSITIVE VERB

I

As the years pass
fewer things remain;
preparing for a journey,
we discard with surprise
much that once seemed necessary.
My last burden is
love; not only for a friend, but for those
whose doors I could never enter.
I cannot comprise the universe
and nothing less will do.
This, I suppose, is why
in a world full of the manifestations of hate
all my poems are about love
(a verb masquerading as a noun
and in search of an object).
But who can hear a fugue
Who's deaf to one note?
Or does a blind man
who once enjoyed paintings
spend his days in an art gallery
in the hope that one of the canvases will become visible?
What sort of mind is this in which.
indifference and love,
stupid and blind,
cohabit?

II

A man is what he does. The heart
is secret and can hurt no one
unless it dictates actions that are wrong.
Treat a child fondly
even from a cold heart; never
love it without sign.
How many of us have
grown out of that
and prefer the reality to the ritual?

It takes even longer to admit
that the deepest love can be
totally unnoticed by its object
or, if noticed,
totally unreturned.

And so for months I watched you
looking casually at me,
and then, after my letter, I watched you
looking casually at me.

The years pass.
And I still must practise,
hour after hour,
being without you.

HOSTESS

Beyond the peopled, empty chairs you stand,
cool, elegant,
a gold Nefertiti;

(the polished glasses in your busy hand
shine uniquely:
I envy their caress);

or, moving like some mad but pleasing island
through roaring, stationary
seas of words,

anticipating some (but what?) demand,
your sunlight body veers
with each capricious wind,
shedding its gold on this or that quicksand,
a warning, or a guide,
to mariners.

And all the time, quite faux-naïfly bland,
your wide eyes speak so loudly
to my heart.

THINKING OF HUGH MACDIARMID

I

Cocooned in cloth, with leather
slapping the stone paving,
he moves his man-high column
of soft flesh, jigsaw bones,
skilfully packaged guts and
pounding blood, improbably
vertical, through acres
of unimportant landscape.

II

What makes a man an instrument?
That people, meeting him, protest
'He wasn't God: he blew his nose!
Tripped on the step! Did *he* write those?'
—'It's an achievement of the mind;
inspired? An idiotic word!' —
While, Chris, your nonsense I respect,
I never doubt your intellect,
but was it only with your intellect
you laid a girl's hand on the *crucifers*?
or saw in the dark sacrifice of roots
the necessary price of beauty? Bards
are judged by what they do, not what they are,
and you, being a materialist, would approve.
Though what you are we love, in what you've done
There's greatness even greater than your own.

III

'In my nature,' said Christopher Smart,
'I quested for beauty,
but God hath sent me to the sea for pearls,'
You've dug since, MacDiarmid,
In many black, wet tunnels,
the detritus of a brutal toil,
hiding your bright body
in a decent Sunday black;
or, edgy in the sun,
have scratched and chipped at hard stone,
clinging to some belief
in case the quarry should appear
only a place and not a thing.
I respect— but don't think I pity it— your condition,
your mind inflamed with metaphor, your lungs choking
with phlegm of parables
and syntax.
What's garnered is plenty and the peril is ephemeral
at the end; a noble end,
to suffer and die among
elusive minerals.
Thinking of Hugh MacDiarmid,
I think of any miner and his shovel.

Thinking of Hugh MacDiarmid,
I think of Yuri Gagarin;
April, '61, near the Aral Sea;
and the slow, meticulous preparation,
all in familiar terms
of mass, escape velocity and thrust;
until a pointer stopped
and the grammar suddenly was transformed.

— How many times, so many years before,
your poems left their floodlit launching gantry
to give to Neptune's icy mask,
to Pluto and enormous Betelgeuse,
'a local habitation and a name.'

Thinking of Hugh MacDiarmid,
I think of Charlie Parker;
the abrupt explosion of style,
the controlled, inventive fertility,
where ideas are sudden, bizarre,
yet no sooner known than familiar;
a continual, instantaneous
interpretation of experience
made possible by a skill
at once mechanical and intellectual.
Thinking of Hugh MacDiarmid,
I think of Christopher Grieve;
with reverence, astonishment,
exasperation, pride, some disapproval,
timidity, delight, a disbelief,
amusement (pardon!), maximum respect,
regrets, gratitude, homage and love.
Thinking of Hugh MacDiarmid,
I think of Christopher Grieve.

BETRAYAL

Voices chatter, but the voice is silent.
Feet clatter, but the foot is still.
Marvels matter, but the marvel is forgotten
　　No tree will drop a leopard on your skull.

Pride preaches, but the racy summer's
Crowded beaches have no room at all.
Love teaches, but it won't forgive you:
　　No one has wound the clock up in the school.

Never mind, for all the world loves you.
Just be kind to dogs, stay out of jail;
Pull down the blind, pretend you haven't noticed
　　The moon at midnight shows each beast its kill.

IMPERFECT

I love you so much
I cannot love you at all.

The emperor's garden
was famous for its roses
but two of the beds
were marred by inferior blooms.
The great stag shot on Tuesday
was a fifteen-pointer, which meant
eight tines on one antler, only
seven on the other.

I love you so much
I cannot love you at all.

A COMEDY

The Echo

It's morning and you walk into my mind,
there for the day,
I cannot say
It's something I expected I should find.

It's not what matters -
these fragments of a haunting air:
eyes a wounding sea has drowned
hunt in my hurt heart now.

(My hand upon the arm
of your chair
and, elegant as a fugue, your knee
so near and yet so many years away.)

The Fawn

I promised a poem to your beauty but only remember
fair hair, dark eyes
and a haunting stillness.

Today I sit
in the fairest place in Scotland,
observing capes and gulls,
the rocks made of rose,
archipelagoes
glittering in the sun.

(A fawn
escapes into the forest
and stands, dappled and listening,
under the cone-dropping trees.)

Tomorrow, at home,
I'll only remember
brown sea, white sand,
and a haunting stillness.

The Words

I give you, girl,
two words.
Shall I put them, like a wafer,
between your lips?
Or with my timid, wary fingers
place them in the palm
of your cool hand?

Perhaps instead
I'll keep them,
count them like an incipient rosary,
or take them out of my pocket
to look at when you're not here.

The Trees

You said 'Tonight' —
I believed you.
Against so much evidence,
I believed you.

Two trees
lean over my heart.
The night passes —
I'm here.
You're where?

Please, friends and relations,
leave me alone.

The Place

The place is something
that you suddenly lose.

All the compromises
You've carefully constructed
over the years, appear irrelevant.

The place is something
you suddenly lose.

If bridges are something
that you burn or cross,

places are something
that you suddenly lose.

THE BRIDGE

Bridges are for crossing.
I looked out
to see if this one
had been blown up in the night.

Chickens are for counting
before they're hatched,
stones are for rolling
where there's no moss,
leaping is for doing
before you look.
This bridge is for burning
before I cross it.

FOLKSONG

Her nose was large —
I was aware of her several imperfections.
The thought of her haunted all my days.

After months of persuasion
she came to my bed.
In the morning, shaving, I asked my mirror: 'And…?'

My girl has a brother.
A nuisance, that one:
he talks vaguely and threateningly about the family's
  honour.

It's absurd to be so critical.
But I wish her breasts were a little fuller, her arms
a little thinner.

It's not bad, you know;
It's not bad…
our bed walks a long way in the night.

DERELICT COTTAGE

You've seen so many like it: the door gone
Long since to make a fire or mend a barrow,
The rooms where earwigs scutter over fragments
Of window glass, bones of small birds, sheep droppings.

'Haunted,' they say. An easy explanation
Of the distress that makes a man aware
(Finding perhaps among the ancient nettles
A doll's head that affection once had fleshed

But blind and brainless in the summer air)
That it's not people do the haunting here,
Rather the purpose of forgotten lives

That lingers in a valley children played in
And Sandwood Bay, a socket in a skull,
Left sightless at the edge of the Atlantic.

FULL CIRCLE

Not two years tall, beginning to be good
Or wicked, when another said he was,
He never knew the moment when he could
Have come to terms with necessary laws.
Perhaps he tore Dad's book or, late at night,
Barefooted in the kitchen ate a cake.
Unfortunately was not caught. The bright
And adult morning found him wide awake.

And so for more than fifty years he fled
Out of the night till, travelling so fast,
He learned the words no-one had ever said
And came back to his origins at last;
And then, a child, stumbled across the floor
And beat his hands on an enormous door.

THE VIEW

A house, bare floors, unfurnished; but the place
In which, next time, we'd meet. I showed you round;
Commented on the merits of more space,
The cost of carpeting, the extra ground
(A nuisance, I agreed, to keep, but wrapped
In privacy the world often denies)
— And all the time my foolish heart was trapped
In your trim body and your dear, shrewd eyes.

Today, I went back there. Jobs to be done —
Books into cupboards, carpets, dishes, brooms.
And then the garden shuddered in the sun.

I stopped a moment to admire the view.
My back was to the window, and the rooms
I had thought empty were all full of you.

SEASONS

Past trees
a girl goes
striding, in a red skirt.

What is more innocent
than a daffodil?
Soft trumpet,
deceptively muted.

Too late,
in autumn,
leaves shout
brass choirs exclaim themselves.

And along the lane an old woman
walks, hirpling,
in her gray clothes.

FROST

'Never seek to tell thy love
Love that never told can be,'
For the heart has barricades
Against its own credulity.

And I learned to my cost
What it means to be alone
With a love construed as lust,
And a folly to atone.

I'd told a young girl all my heart
And she, laughing, said to me:
'Love is for the young and gay —
You are far too old for me.'

And I shivered with a frost
Many a manly man has known,
And my blood turned into dust
And my heart became a stone.

THE OLD WOMAN

The old woman —
face like a slab.
Eyes of flat stone
still closed under open lids.
Look at them, and you
are a moment years ago, a
speck of dust, or a cry
made between beating of a gull's wings.
Hours pass,
silently, through her knotted fists.
Nothing matters: you, death, her.
I don't really believe it.
Can no anguish of my fading youth
make her face crack with more than wrinkles?
Can I not take her hands; say
'Listen, dear… ' ?

TU FU from FU TU

Tu Fu, my friend and colleague,
mutters to himself
over little amber glasses;
hammers with heavy, hurt fingers
on his new and quaking typewriter.

Pain can batter through to meaning.

I sit
looking glumly at the dull grate,
wanting to talk;
not with words
but with music to a perceptive,
if not too critical, listener;
or better,
with the eloquence of lips and arms
—a technique I once nearly mastered.

THE ANGLER

Casting a line at random I have caught
A little shining April with silver scales,
The latest and most precious ever drawn
Splashing and kicking to the surface of green Time.
And other pasts lie heavy in my creel,
Secure and dead in the remembering air —
The wary August and the record June.
They were my triumphs, would amaze my friends,
But lie forgotten now the sun illumes
The sparkling sequins of this little month
— That is too small to keep and takes its life
Back to the water where my memories drown.

TO A SON, LEAVING TO GO TO THE UNIVERSITY

You turned towards another town
To study how to stop being young,
And as you closed the door I called:
'Don't go too far; don't stay too long.'

Hearts don't grow wise for being old.
Did I forget that I must go
So soon to such a farther land
Than your young years begin to know?

I hope, in that reluctant hour
When I move with the shadowy throng,
To hear your voice, once only, say:
'Don't go too far; don't stay too long.'

STILL

The still of cliffs,
immoveable,
(though silently eroding).
The still of tides, unwinded,
drifting
on to the reflective sand.
There is another still —
expressed into bottles,
spring-fed into small receptive glasses,
that makes beauty bearable,
its absence almost endurable.

INTERRUPTIONS

The little girl opened her hand
and fourteen flamingos flew into the air —

O trumpets and gay ophicleides!
when will your melodious march be equalled?
I walked under the trees with a book
opened at page
eleven,
it was about aerodynamics,
a subject in which I take a moderate interest —

but the little girl opened her hand
and fourteen flamingos flew into the air.

SOUTHERN PASTORAL

A black song from blind eyes; rain
shivers on the branch.
A tree leans, delicately, this
afternoon of destruction.

Faces sweat-gilt:
Jake, Larry, Butch —
'all changed, changed utterly' —
in the sweet and guilty air.

The smell of magnolia
and singeing flesh;
and an old tree, bending
under a new weight.

COMFORT

Don't have in your house
comfort for guest:
he'll make you the visitor,
then his slave.

He'll fill your dreams with sawdust,
cracking his ruthless soft whip;
he'll lull you to sleep and stand
jeering at your poor noble body.

Your wiser judgements will be mocked,
treated like delicate toys,
comfort will kill your passions
and appear, grinning, at the funeral.

(after Kahlil Gibran)

A LITTLE ACID FOR OUR DADS

The years would be our masters,
We knew it even then;
Though, flushed with youth and folly,
We never reckoned when.

The Earth was peopled only
With folk whom we could trust,
And Time we'd come to terms with
Or founder, if we must.

We nourished our resistance
In crannies and in nooks
And, hidden from the adults,
Read the forbidden books,

And, pushing back the nightmare,
Appeared to play the game;
Knowing that to be honest
Would not be quite the same.

But, nibbling at the edges
Of our embattled pride,
Were regiments of traitors
We should have kept outside.

Their faces were familiar:
Nanny's, or even Mum's;
The dear and cosy uncles
Who wanted to be chums.

We noticed lonely aunties —
Sad victims of the time —
Whose lives, broken and wasted,
Had paid for the sublime

Impertinent assumption
That Truth and Honour lay
In catalogues and folders
Quite neatly filed away

Until the dreaded audits
Were annually made,
And nobody was laughing,
No one was unafraid.

(And, with sardonic hindsight,
It's really rather funny
To think the LSD
Might earlier have been money).

We don't know what you took
To expiate your guilt,
We hope it was effective
And none of it was spilt.

Your various devices
To hide your awful slip,
We've paid for. But we hope
You had a pleasant trip.

THE EXILE

Know in his voice the unforgiven exile
To whom our manners are a polite joke,
And eyes of strangers clocks upon the wall;
See in his eyes our fear has left a mark.
Learn by his love the lonely fruitful journey
From this today his traitor wisdom made;
But do not ask him why he had to hurry,
Or where he went, or was he not afraid.

Learning so quickly he could never know
Why all he loved had to be left behind.
He wished he had not been the one to go,
It was bad luck. He had not thought to find
Heaven a desert, or discover how
Truth is more sad than any man knows now.

THE POET

He never mastered destiny. The land
He stumbled on had rushed across the sea
Into his stunned horizon: fortune and
Compliance made him part of history.
The continent elected him a god,
Who could not read a compass or the stars
And had in desperation gone abroad
To seek escape from inter-tribal wars.

The crown they gave him did not fit, his laws
Were laughed at. But the nincompoop was flattered
To think that half the world now bore his name.
Biographers were kind to him because
The world was half the size before he came.
And that, not he, was all that really mattered.

NOTES

WHO WALKS WITH PLOVER
When he wrote this, Crombie Saunders believed that 'plover' rhymed with 'clover', and was most annoyed thereafter to discover it in fact rhymes with 'lover'. (See also *The Empty Glen*).

ABOVE THE FORMIDABLE TOMB
'<u>For</u>midable' and '<u>la</u>mentable' – the stress on the first syllable of course.

THE EMPTY GLEN
Can be found in two anthologies: Maurice Lindsay (ed.) *Modern Scottish Poetry: 1925-1985* (London: Robert Hale, 1986). Maurice Lindsay & Lesley Duncan (ed.) *The Edinburgh Book of Twentieth Century Scottish Verse* (Edinburgh: Edinburgh University Press, 2005).

THE PANTHERS
Published in Douglas Young (ed.) *Scottish Verse, 1951-1951* (Edinburgh: Thomas Nelson & Son, 1952).

SONNET
Published in Douglas Young (ed.) *Scottish Verse, 1951-1951* (Edinburgh: Thomas Nelson & Son, 1952).

AN ELEGY FOR THE GLORY AND THE DREAM
The title refers to Wordsworth's ode 'Intimations of Immortality from Recollections of Early Childhood':

Whither is fled the visionary gleam?
Where is it now, the glory and the dream?

In *The Year's Green Edge*, the title of this poem is given as

'The Year's Green Edge'. I have reverted to the original title. 'Raspberries' – when the comic associations were pointed out to him, Crombie Saunders toyed with the idea of replacing this with 'daffodils', but reverted to *le mot juste.*

HAD I TWA HERTS
'Twin'd' – Scots for 'separated'. Nothing to do with 'entwined'.

THE HAMECOMIN
From Hölderlin's 'Die Heimat' (not, as the title might suggest, the longer poem, 'Heimkunft').

DOUN THE WATTIR WI THE LAVE
The writers specifically referred to are, in order of appearance: Douglas Young, Hugh MacDiarmid, Alexander Scott, Sydney Goodsir Smith and Maurice Lindsay. Lindsay was reportedly furious when this was pointed out to him. That he cut back Crombie Saunders's contributions in later editions of *Modern Scottish Poetry* may be coincidental.

'Alang the bank a poetess...' – Edith Sitwell, an early champion of Goodsir Smith's work. By 1857 she had acquired four honorary doctorates 'to put on her luggage labels' and used them all, something Crombie Saunders found risibly pretentious ('a DLitt tae!').

For a thoroughly contemporary poem this has venerable antecedents. The form is that of 'Christis Kirk of the Green' (circa 1500) and the even earlier 'Peblis to the Play'.

ECHOES
Published in A*kros*, IV, no. 11 (1969).

THE ENCOUNTER
The poet noted: 'I'm afraid the first poem in the collection, from which the title is taken, is very 'romantic'. But the image presented itself so forcibly I hadn't the temerity to query its credentials.'

WALKING ALONE IN THE DREAM-LONGED CITY
Some lines here are taken from an earlier poem, 'In the
Loneliness of a Classic Dispensation', published in the USA
in 1944 (*Contemporary Poetry*, Baltimore, Maryland) but
omitted from the collections:

In the loneliness of a classic dispensation
I hanker after old gods,
Seeing behind the crooner and the comic strip
The twitching eyelids of those who are alone in cities.
Finding in memory's hygienic dust-bin
The broken doll that was not to be discarded,
The toy drum filled with soldiers, the ghost in the
    wardrobe,
Sea-war and shipwreck on the garage steps…

REVENGE
The first line quotes 'Song' by Christina Rossetti:

And if thou wilt, remember,
And if thou wilt, forget.

Published in *Poor Old Tired Horse,* issue 3.

JANET AT THE SEASIDE
Published in *Poor Old Tired Horse,* issue 7.

THINKING OF HUGH MACDIARMID
This was one of the poems in a collection presented
to MacDiarmid on the occasion of his 75th birthday.
The quote, 'a local habitation…' is from A Midsummer
Night's Dream, Act V, Scene 1: ' …the poet's pen
turns them to shapes, and gives to aery nothing
a local habitation and a name.' 'In my nature… – from
Christopher Smart, 'Jubilate Agno'.

IMPERFECT
Published in Norman MacCaig & Alexander Scott (ed.) *Contemporary Scottish Verse, 1959-69* (Edinburgh: Calder Publications, 1970).

DERELICT COTTAGE
Published in Norman MacCaig & Alexander Scott (ed.) *Contemporary Scottish Verse, 1959-69* (Edinburgh: Calder Publications, 1970).

FROST
The initial quotations is from William Blake.

TU FU from FU TU
'Tu Fu' – Alasdair Thompson, a fellow English Teacher at McLaren High, Callander. He was also an occasional poet (author, 'Persons and Places').

TO A SON, LEAVING TO GO TO THE UNIVERSITY
This poem is complimented by W S Graham in a letter to Saunders. See Michael & Margaret Snow (ed.) *The Night-fisherman: selected letters of W S Graham* (Manchester: Carcanet, 1999), pp 326-327.

INTERRUPTIONS
Published in Norman MacCaig & Alexander Scott (ed.) *Contemporary Scottish Verse, 1959-69* (Edinburgh: Calder Publications, 1970). Ophicleides are trumpet-like brass instruments.

SOUTHERN COMFORT
Published in *Akros*, V, no. 15 (1970).

GLOSSARY

adventur (Middle Scots)................. chance, accident
alluterlie (Middle Scots) ....completely

ballant-buiks .... poetry books
bien...comfortable
biggs .... builds
brukkil (Middle Scots)......................... brittle, fragile

carlin..................................... here, man (derogatory)
ches .... chosen
cowpan.. overturning
crines .... shrinks, shrivels
cuddy ....horse

darna ....daren't
dolour.. sorrow, grief
doucelik .... sober, sedate
dree... suffer
dwynit.................................... drooped, wasted away

eident ....busy, diligent
endlang .... along
erd.. earth

faurben..far off
ferlie .... wonder, marvel
fordelyd .... extravagant
forouten ....outside of
forpleynit.. lamenting

gantit .... yawned
gaw ....blemish, hurt
graifen-stede .... cemetery
grame ....anger, distress
grue .... shudder (with fear, repulsion)

hantle ....a good deal
hapt..wrapped, clad
herts.. hearts
hummle..submit

kimmer.................................. a lass; a married woman

lave ....rest
laverock .... lark
leit lichtlie...............................esteem little
lemanrie.................................... love affair
liggs .... lies
lyft... sky

mensefou .... decorous

orra ....various

preclair (Middle Scots) .... bright, splendid
puirtith... poverty

remeid ....remedy
rengan .... ruling
ressaif (Middle Scots)...receive

saikless..innocent
saul ....soul
servitour (Middle Scots)................................ servant
screivit.. written
shilpit .... pinched, emaciated
siller...money (silver)
skaith...injury
smirr...................................... fine rain, drizzle
speird .... asked (for)
steekit.. closed
sterns, sternies .... stars
sweirt.. reluctant

trowless...faithless
tuim ....empty
twa-thrie ....several
twin'd...parted

walken... awaken
wame...belly
weel-faurd .... handsome, good looking
wicht... fellow, bloke
winnock .... window

RYMOUR BOOKS

POETRY · HISTORY · DEBATE